C000072277

Free Yourself from the IRS

Relieve Your Stress,
Reduce What You Owe,
and Regain Your Freedom

Jesus Zacarias Abikarram

Free Yourself from the IRS

Relieve Your Stress, Reduce What You Owe, and Regain Your Freedom

ISBN (paperback): 978-1-956220-03-2

ISBN (hardcover): 978-1-956220-12-4

Disclaimer

This publication is designed to provide accurate and authoritative information regarding the subject matter contained within. It should be understood that the author and publisher are not engaged in rendering legal, accounting, or other financial service through this medium. The author and publisher shall not be liable for your misuse of this material and shall have neither liability nor responsibility to anyone with respect to any loss or damage caused or alleged to be caused, directly or indirectly, by the information contained in this book. The author and/or publisher do not guarantee that anyone following these strategies, suggestions, tips, ideas, or techniques will become successful. If legal advice or other expert assistance is required, the services of a competent professional should be sought.

Expert Press

www.ExpertPress.net

Table of Contents

Section III:

Chapter 7

Chapter 8

Chapter 9

DEDICATION

This book is dedicated to my mother, Dolores Espino, who always guided us to become the best in our endeavors; to my wife, Lourdes; my children, Katherine, Anais, and Kayla; my brothers, Jose Agustin and Jose Alberto; and my sister, Karen, for their persistent encouragement to always do better. Last (but not least), this is dedicated to my father, Zacarias Abikarram, who always made sure I stayed in line, working honorably and fairly to serve those in need.

TESTIMONIALS

"Jesus and his team are amazing. I had let my taxes go unfiled for years, and they caught me up, then handled issues with the IRS and Marketplace for the ACA on my behalf. They made my stressful experience anything but. I am all caught up and even got fairly substantial refunds."

—Sharon M.

"Highly recommended for all your tax issues, especially tax-problem resolution."

—Antonio Nava, Enrolled Agent

"Great customer service. The team at Freedom Tax Resolution is reliable, knowledgeable, and professional."

—Norma E.

"Very professional and friendly. Always willing to serve the customer, doesn't matter the time of the day, and very knowledgeable."

—Alejandro B.

"*Due to travel and other distractions last year, I missed the deadline for requesting extensions for two of my corporations. Even though there was no tax due, the penalties were severe. I gave the notices to Jesus, and he immediately sent letters to the IRS, demonstrating 'reasonable cause' and saving me over $3,600 in penalties.*"

—Bob W.

INTRODUCTION

For nearly 250 years, the words *freedom* and *America* have been so closely linked as to seem almost synonymous. With rights such as freedom of the press, freedom of religion, and freedom of speech, our Founding Fathers created a system of government founded on the principle that no such system should be more powerful than the citizens being governed. Yet every year, tens of thousands of Americans find themselves imprisoned—not literally but financially— by the vast bureaucratic monolith that is the United States Internal Revenue Service. Shackled to a debt that seems overwhelming and unconquerable, the taxpaying citizens of a country known for its freedoms are facing wage garnishments, liens, and levies, and sometimes even the loss of their homes—all without knowing that *it doesn't have to be like this.*

For every IRS tax problem, there is a tax resolution. My name is Jesus Abikarram, and I'm a Tax Resolution Specialist. In *Free Yourself from the IRS: Relieve Your Stress, Reduce What You Owe, and Regain Your Freedom,* I'll debunk the more common myths associated with the IRS, show you how and why you may have wound up in the government's crosshairs, and explain your rights and options. Above all, I'll demonstrate how your right to representation is the last right you ever want to waive.

As they say, "Knowledge is power." At approximately 75,000 pages, the US tax code is one of the lengthiest and most constantly evolving government documents. Unless you've spent years (or, in my case, decades) studying it, there's simply no way to understand the best way to use it to your advantage. There's certainly no single book with all the answers.

This book, rather, is meant to be a guide to discovering how to find the answers—whether you're a taxpayer facing garnishment or levy, a friend or relative of such a taxpayer, or a CPA or other professional tasked with serving such taxpayers. Throughout, you'll notice I never refer to "clients" or "customers"; I don't use those words. They're all taxpayers to me—taxpayers with whom I work closely to *relieve their stress, reduce what they owe, and regain their freedom.*

You'll also notice I give out my phone number a lot—it's (833) IRS-ISSUE or (833) 477-4778—and I welcome you to call me. If you see this as overly self-aggrandizing or self-promotional, that's not my intent. First and foremost, I see my job as helping people. Calling me is the best way to get my help.

If the information provided in this book gives you some insight into your tax situation that helps you resolve it without coming to me, I've succeeded.

Section I:

Knowledge Is Power

Chapter 1

The Making of a Tax Resolution Specialist

I often get asked, "Why do you do it?"

It's an understandable question. My stock answer is usually, "People need help. I like to help people." What's often actually meant is, "What in the world would make someone want to deal with the IRS on purpose? For a living?" My stock answer still applies, but obviously there's more to it than that.

Most boys—including immigrant boys raised in New York City (I moved to the United States from the Dominican Republic when I was a one-year-old)—grow up with dreams of becoming athletes or firefighters or policemen or entertainers. Few aspire to one day becoming a tax resolution specialist (TRS).

Neither did I. In fact, there was no such thing as a TRS until the 1980s, when a few enterprising entrepreneurs did some research into the thousands of pages of the IRS Revenue Code and discovered tax relief opportunities for individuals and business owners. Many people, including a surprising number of CPAs and tax attorneys, didn't have a clue.

And an industry was born.

Sadly, this fledgling industry was quickly overrun by scam artists offering to "buy your IRS debt." As is often the case with endeavors based on even the noblest of principles, the entire profession was tainted with a mistrust usually reserved for the IRS itself. The Federal Trade Commission stepped in during the nineties and levied huge damages against many of the perpetrators of such scams. The bad apples haven't disappeared entirely, but they're now by far the exception. (That being said, always do your research. Read up. Buying this book is a good start.)

As I see it (and as I practice it), tax resolution isn't simply about helping people. It has its roots in one of this nation's most cherished documents: the Declaration of Independence. I've been in love with the "D of I" since a third-grade field trip to Philadelphia. I spent half my lunch money on a copy, printed on one of the city's original presses. I still have it, framed, adorning the wall of my office and every office I've ever had, beginning in 1993.

I'm not sure exactly what it was about these wise words that so captivated an eight-year-old's imagination. I think it was partly the "all Men are created equal" line and partly the "unalienable Rights, that among these are Life, Liberty, and the Pursuit of Happiness" line. That it was also our Founding Fathers' way of telling a king to get bent probably made an impression too. Talk about standing up to authority!

We all know that one of the primary beefs the colonies had with England was "taxation without representation." The colonies were referencing the imposition of taxes on citizens without giving them a say-so in the matter. Over the course of my career, however, I came to see this concept in another light. Those who are taxed have the right to representation *after* the taxes are levied. This seems perfectly in line with the spirit of the Declaration—having your property seized or your wages garnished definitely qualifies as a hindrance to life, liberty, and the pursuit of happiness.

As unlikely as it may seem, my journey to becoming a TRS began when I became an auto insurance broker in 1992. The next year, in February 1993, I got my first office: a 400-square-foot space in a building owned by the Archdiocese of New York. I spent $3,000 on a computer (one of the first made available for the public to purchase), and my father didn't speak to me for a month. He thought I'd bought an expensive toy.

Later that same year, I partnered with my brother Jose Austin, who was in accounting and had opened up a small insurance agency. We needed someone to handle tax issues. I've always been methodical and detail oriented, so I thought I could fill the bill. My brother insisted I get properly trained and said the words I tell clients to this very day:

"You have to know what you're doing. When these things get done wrong, people get in trouble."

So in 1993, I took the tax preparation course, passed the test, and registered with the IRS as a tax preparer. With personal computers still in their infancy, I grew tired of various programmers and service techs taking advantage of me. So in 1996, I got my associate degree in computer science from Monroe College.

Through the course of my job, I developed an interest in tax and insurance fraud and subsequently received a bachelor of science degree in security management from the John Jay College of Criminal Justice in 2003. Although I didn't become a fraud investigator (an idea with which I'd briefly flirted), what I learned about investigative techniques has helped immensely in my role as a TRS.

That computer science degree has come in pretty handy too.

In 2004, I was ready for a change of scenery. I left New York and moved to South Florida, opening an office in Hallandale Beach, near Miami.

While I derived great pleasure from helping people prepare their taxes, I found myself wanting to branch out, to get more involved with those who found themselves facing the consequences of being in significant debt to the IRS. In other words, people in trouble—usually as a result of not having their taxes properly prepared in the first place. (We'll discuss the pitfalls of the "box store" tax preparers in another chapter.) So I decided to become an enrolled agent (EA), one of the few groups of people, along with CPAs and tax attorneys, authorized to represent people before the IRS.

To say that it's easier to become a tax preparer than an EA is like saying it's easier to get your driver's license than to become an airline pilot. I'm proud to say that I passed all three of the highly intense tests on the first try. That's rare. It's not because I'm smarter. I think it's just because I love this stuff. I'm the kind of guy who reads tax codes for fun. Because I like helping people, it's a win-win for me. Thanks to the internet age and being licensed in all fifty states, I'm able to help people anywhere in the United States.

As a member of the National Association of Enrolled Agents, the National Association of Tax Professionals, and the American Society of Tax Problem Solvers, I keep up with the fluid and constantly evolving US tax code. I always notify the taxpayers my company serves (past and present) of changes that can affect them.

At the end of the day, what we want to do is get you tax compliant at as little cost as legally possible and help you avoid having a lien, levy, or garnishment filed against you.

It's all about helping people.

As I've mentioned, that's why I do it.

Chapter 2

The IRS Taxpayer Bill of Rights

If you know much about the US Constitution (I've studied it extensively and keep a copy at both my home and office), you know that the Bill of Rights—the first ten amendments—was ratified shortly after the Constitution itself. In fact, James Madison wanted to incorporate the amendments into the Constitution. He was outvoted on that one.

The IRS, which wasn't established until the Civil War, took a little bit longer to come up with its own Bill of Rights. Okay, a lot longer—over 150 years! Actually, taxpayer rights were already in the tax code; they were just scattered throughout its thousands of pages and largely unknown to the public. In 2014, National Taxpayer Advocate Nina Olson (she headed the Taxpayer Advocate Service, the IRS's internal watchdog group) found that "most taxpayers do not believe they have rights before the IRS and even fewer can name their rights."[1] The IRS bundled these rights together and created the Taxpayer Bill of Rights, which is now not only provided to every taxpayer but is also required reading for every IRS employee.

In this chapter, we're going to examine the Taxpayer Bill of Rights.[2] I'll show you exactly what it says, but—more importantly—I'll tell you what it *doesn't* say.

1. The Right to Be Informed

Taxpayers have the right to know what they need to do to comply with the tax laws. They are entitled to clear explanations of the laws and IRS procedures in all tax forms, instructions, publications, notices, and correspondence. They have the right to be informed of IRS decisions about their tax accounts and to receive clear explanations of the outcomes.

This basically says that you have the right to know what's going on and what needs to be done in order to comply. You also have the right to know what forms to use in order to become compliant and what the outcome may be if you fail to do so (like wage garnishments, levies, or property seizures). The IRS will often give you a deadline to become compliant. Failure to act by this

---

1 Nina E. Olson, "IRS Adopts 'Taxpayer Bill of Rights;' 10 Provisions to be Highlighted on IRS.gov, in Publication 1," IR-2014-72, June 10, 2014, https://www.irs.gov/newsroom/is-adopts-taxpayer-bill-of-rights-10-provisions-to-be-highlighted-on-irsgov-in-publication-1.

2 "Taxpayer Bill of Rights." Internal Revenue Service. Accessed September 9, 2021. https://www.irs.gov/taxpayer-bill-of-rights.

deadline is often tantamount to admitting guilt and accepting the consequences.

The term "clear explanations" (and you'll notice it's used twice) often has taxpayers scratching their heads. Clear to whom?

Well, clear to me. But I'm a tax professional. It's one thing to tell a taxpayer *what* they need to do. If you're counting on the IRS to explain *how* to do it—or which of the over eight hundred forms and schedules are an exact fit for your particular situation—you'll be spinning your wheels. That can cost you. If you submit the wrong form (or fill it out incorrectly), it will be rejected.

That can cost you too.

2. The Right to Quality Service

Taxpayers have the right to receive prompt, courteous, and professional assistance in their dealings with the IRS, to be spoken to in a way they can easily understand, to receive clear and easily understandable communications from the IRS, and to have a way to file complaints about inadequate service.

This one came about, in part, because of complaints about IRS employees treating taxpayers like second-class citizens. It's the reason any IRS agent you speak with will provide their name and badge number at the beginning of the conversation.

"Prompt" doesn't mean you won't wait on the phone for three hours before the conversation actually begins. It means that the IRS will process the forms you've submitted properly as soon as they've processed the case before yours. "Prompt" is another one of those things, like "clear and easily understandable communications," that is in the eye of the beholder. And, in this case, the beholder is the IRS.

3. The Right to Pay No More Than the Correct Amount of Tax

> Taxpayers have the right to pay only the amount of tax legally due, including interest and penalties, and to have the IRS apply all tax payments properly.

This one is a little misleading. That line about "including interest and penalties" means you will pay whatever the IRS says you owe, and they get it wrong. They're human. If I told you that they err in favor of the taxpayer as often as they err in favor of themselves, I'd be lying. Errors in favor of the taxpayer are exceedingly rare.

And while they tell you up front (per the first clause, "the right to be informed") what the interest and penalties will be, most taxpayers have no idea how quickly and significantly these can add up to disaster. As a tax resolution specialist, it's my job to A) make sure the original amount owed is correct (through a thorough analysis of your tax situation), and B) use my expertise and experience to reduce or even eliminate the interest and penalties (including, but not limited to, what's known as "penalty abatement").

We'll talk more about this, and I'll show you some real-life examples later in the book.

4. The Right to Challenge the IRS's Position and Be Heard

> Taxpayers have the right to raise objections and provide additional documentation in response to formal IRS actions or proposed actions, to expect that the IRS will consider their timely objections and documentation promptly and fairly, and to receive a response if the IRS does not agree with their position.

This is all well and good, except that raising those objections and providing additional documentation has to be done in a very specific way, using very specific forms. Any mistake or variation from strict protocol will result in your objections/documentation being rejected.

It can be a nightmare. If I had written the IRS Taxpayer Bill of Rights, I would have added "Don't try this at home." I probably would have put that at the top.

5. The Right to Appeal an IRS Decision in an Independent Forum

Taxpayers are entitled to a fair and impartial administrative appeal of most IRS decisions, including many penalties, and have the right to receive a written response regarding the Office of Appeals' decision. Taxpayers generally have the right to take their cases to court.

There's an old saying, perhaps most famously (although not definitively) attributed to Abraham Lincoln, that states, "A man who represents himself has a fool for a client." Perhaps that's a bit harsh, but I will say that I've never seen such a case come out well, both in court proceedings and IRS appeals, where the taxpayer attempted to handle it on their own. I'm sure there are exceptions.

But here's the deal: It's exceedingly rare that it ever comes to that. Every once in a great while, an IRS agent I've been dealing with will refuse to budge, and I'll have to go (or telecommute) to an IRS Appeals Office. I'll request that a supervisor be present. Again, this hardly ever happens, but if it needs to happen, it will. I don't take no for an answer. I won't even take on a case unless I know I can get something better for the taxpayer than what the IRS is demanding.

As of this writing, I have a 100 percent acceptance rate from the IRS on offers I've made on behalf of the taxpayers I help. In many cases (some of which I'll detail later) that offer has been zero dollars.

6. The Right to Finality

Taxpayers have the right to know the maximum amount of time they have to challenge the IRS's position as well as the maximum amount of time the IRS has to audit a particular tax year. Taxpayers have the right to know when the IRS has finished an audit.

This is basically the IRS acknowledging statutes of limitation. While most audits begin a few months after you file, they technically have up to three years to charge you additional taxes. This is known as the "assessment statute of limitations." Rarely does it take that long. The IRS manual states that agents should be closing audits within twenty-six months.

The audits that begin the quickest usually involve claimed tax credits on returns where a refund is due, mainly because the IRS has to pay interest on refunds that are held up. Other types of audits—where the IRS is claiming money owed to them—generally begin within about a year of the filing date.

Once a tax debt is assessed, the IRS has ten years to collect. A couple of caveats here: If a payment arrangement has been made, each payment "resets" that ten-year statute of limitations; and if they file a lien against you in court, they have the right to renew the lien for another ten years. Just two of many reasons why you need someone like me on your side.

7. The Right to Privacy

Taxpayers have the right to expect that any IRS inquiry, examination, or enforcement action will comply with the law and be no more intrusive than necessary and will respect all due process rights, including search and seizure protections and a collection due process hearing where applicable.

This one ties in with the original Bill of Rights—the Fourth Amendment, to be precise. But it goes further than that. The IRS is limited as to what they can seize or how much of your wages they can garnish. They can't take your primary residence without a court order, and they can't take so much of your paycheck that you can't afford to pay your other bills.

8. The Right to Confidentiality

Taxpayers have the right to expect that any information they provide to the IRS will not be disclosed unless authorized by the taxpayer or by law. Taxpayers have the right to expect the IRS to investigate and take appropriate action against its employees, return preparers, and others who wrongfully use or disclose taxpayer return information.

This one sounds like it could have been included in number seven. But then, they would have only had nine clauses. I'm fairly certain that had nothing to do with it.

When your case is assigned to an IRS agent, they're not allowed to discuss it with other agents, except their supervisors. Likewise, they can't inform any other creditors you may have about what they're doing. They also don't have the right to share your information with other government entities (like your state tax assessor).

They're serious about this stuff. Loose lips get pink slips.

9. The Right to Retain Representation

Taxpayers have the right to retain an authorized representative of their choice to represent them in their dealings with the IRS. Taxpayers have the right to be told that if they cannot afford to hire a representative, they may be eligible for assistance from a Low Income Taxpayer Clinic.

This almost seems like a taxpayer Miranda warning.

As I mentioned earlier, there are only three types of professionals allowed to represent you before the IRS: tax attorneys, CPAs, and enrolled agents (like me). While there may be times when you're justified spending the extra money on one of the first two, it's almost always in your best interest to come to me first. Indeed, many tax attorneys and CPAs come to me themselves. Their fields of expertise are broader, and they're not required to undergo such intensive testing on many facets that may apply more specifically to your case.

10. The Right to a Fair and Just Tax System

Taxpayers have the right to expect the tax system to consider facts and circumstances that might affect their underlying liabilities, ability to pay, or ability to provide information timely. Taxpayers have the right to receive assistance from the Taxpayer Advocate Service if they are experiencing financial difficulty or if the IRS has not resolved their tax issues properly and timely through its normal channels.

This last clause of the IRS Taxpayer Bill of Rights tells us that they understand that every situation is unique and that they're willing to consider your unique circumstances. It's a little misleading because—I promise you—whatever your special circumstance or situation is, they're going to have a form for it.

The Taxpayer Advocate Service (independent from the IRS, like the Appeals Office) is a last resort. They're somewhat choosy about the cases they take on. If you haven't done absolutely everything possible (and done it correctly) to resolve your situation with the IRS, they'll simply send you back to the IRS. The IRS will most likely give you yet another form. Like the Appeals Office, the Taxpayer Advocate Service is something the taxpayers I serve almost never need.

Now you know your rights. As you can probably tell, there's a big difference between knowing your rights and understanding your rights. There's an even bigger difference between understanding them and applying them in a way that ensures total resolution at the lowest possible cost.

That's why you have me.

Chapter 3

Debunking IRS Myths

Everywhere you look these days, there's either misinformation or *dis*information. When it comes to the IRS, most of the inaccuracies fall into the former category. They're wrong but not intentionally wrong.

They're just myths.

Most IRS myths surround the filing of taxes rather than audits, simply because far more people file than get audited. Yet, clearly, it's the myths about filing that can get you audited.

Myths can be expensive.

In this chapter, I'll talk about a few of the most prevalent myths.

Myth #1: "I don't make enough money for the IRS to pay attention."

This is a common myth that gets a lot of people in trouble.

According to data from the IRS, you have about the same chance (approximately one-half of 1 percent) of being audited if you make less than $25,000 per year than if you make $250,000 per year. That percentage rises above 1 percent when your income passes the half-million mark, but that's because taxpayers in the higher brackets generally have the most complex returns and, therefore, a greater possibility of errors. And, frankly, these high earners usually have a greater incentive to try to get out of paying what they rightfully owe. This is in no way meant to disparage the wealthy; it's merely an observation based on statistics. Look at it this way. If a million people underpay by fifty dollars, that's $50 million that lawfully belongs to the IRS. The IRS is going to collect it.

Simply put, the IRS is looking for discrepancies, not income. We'll cover this more in the next section.

Myth #2: "If I electronically file my tax returns, I have a greater chance of being audited."

We live in the digital age. The majority of IRS tax returns (about 73 percent overall, nearly 90 percent for individual taxpayers) are filed electronically. This is a good thing. This is why we get our refunds so much more quickly than we used to. Yet there are many who fear that filing electronically isn't as safe as doing it the old-fashioned way. In reality, the opposite is true.

One way or another, your tax returns will be filed electronically and uploaded into the IRS database. Sending your return in by mail means that an IRS employee will be entering in the information. You're adding a human element that would otherwise be bypassed. While it can be said that computers will often catch something that a real person might miss, it can also work the other way around. And you're not going to catch a computer having a bad day.

Myth #3: "I don't need to send the IRS a detailed report."

Many are under the mistaken impression that they can guesstimate certain deductions or that there is an "allowable" deduction for things like having a home office or health care. They don't believe they need to show proof.

This is just wrong.

Yes, there are maximum deductions for all sorts of things, but that doesn't mean you're allowed to automatically deduct that amount. Doing this is a surefire way to get yourself an audit. If you deduct it, you must be able to show it. You need your receipts or bank statements, and they need to be itemized. If the deduction is over $200, you need both your receipt and proof of source of payment (usually the bank statement).

As a tax resolution specialist, part of the investigation phase involves helping the taxpayers I serve gather up evidence for the deductions they've claimed. I usually find some errors. Often, however, I also find items that could have been deducted but weren't.

I really like that part.

Myth #4: "If I'm self-employed, I run a greater risk of being audited."

Not necessarily.

This kind of goes back to the need for detailed reporting. It's not the fact that you're self-employed that raises red flags with the IRS, it's that your return will be more complicated and therefore more prone to errors. This is especially true if you're filing a Schedule C as a sole proprietor. In this case, in the eyes of the IRS, you and your business are the same entity. As I'm sure you can imagine (or if you're a sole proprietor, already know), the line between business and personal expenses can sometimes be blurred. And, especially if much of your business is done in cash, sometimes things can fall through the cracks. This might be purely by accident or the result of poor record keeping and documentation, or it might be the result of some "creative accounting" combined with the wishful thinking that the IRS won't notice.

They will.

Myth #5: "The IRS is going to take everything I own and put me in prison."

First of all, no one in America goes to jail for owing money. You can go to jail for tax fraud, but there's an amazingly high burden of proof placed on the government to show intent. It's very rare.

Second, yes, the government can take your home or your car or your boat. They can seize your assets. They can garnish your wages. They can even take your passport. We'll talk more about some of this, and how to avoid these situations, later.

The bottom line is that these are all last resorts. I promise you: IRS agents are not villains diabolically working behind the scenes to leave you homeless and broke. They only want the money they're rightfully owed. It's how we finance our government.

Myth #6: "If I use a paid tax preparer, I'm less likely to get audited."

That would be nice if it were true. It's not.

The IRS's computer system makes no distinction whatsoever between a return you did yourself and one you hired someone to do for you. They only look for discrepancies. The sad truth is that studies by both the Government Accountability Office and the IRS itself found that returns prepared by paid tax preparers actually had more errors than those prepared by the taxpayers themselves.

There are a couple of reasons for this. In most cases, it's because the taxpayer provided incorrect information.

But you also have to realize that many tax preparers base their reputations (and their marketing) on their ability to get you a big refund, so they have an incentive to err on the side of their customers. The studies bear this out. (Note: If you receive a greater refund than you're entitled to, you will have to pay back the overage to the IRS.)

While I'm all for having a good tax preparer, I'm not a big fan of these places that only pop up at tax time, often in Walmart or in tiny offices in strip malls. Most states don't have set licensing requirements for such tax preparers (the federal government only requires that they have a "Preparer Tax Identification Number," or PTIN), so their training can be minimal. These places are kind of the "McDonald's" of tax preparation. They're fast, they're cheap, and there's a chance they'll get your order wrong.

The tax preparer industry is also rife with fraud. You can google "tax preparer fraud" and see page after page of cases of unscrupulous so-called tax "professionals" who have bilked both the IRS and their customers. Here are a few things that should raise a red flag:

- Your tax preparer asks you to authorize your return before you've had a chance to review it.

- Your tax preparer asks you to sign a blank tax form (which seems like a no-brainer, but it happens).

- Your tax preparer asks you to authorize having your refund deposited into *their* account.

Do your due diligence. One good source of information is the IRS's Directory of Federal Tax Return Preparers with Credentials and Select Qualifications, available online. It's not the most exciting read, but it can save you some headaches.

These are only a few of the more common myths surrounding the IRS. If you're reading this book, it may be a case of hindsight being 20/20. You very well may already be getting audited or have otherwise found yourself in trouble with the IRS.

This is where I come in.

Section II:

How You Got Here

Chapter 4

The Dreaded Letters

You filed your federal tax return. You either received your refund or paid the amount you owed. You breathe a sigh of relief, secure in the knowledge that you and the IRS are all square and that you won't even have to think about taxes until next year. It's a great feeling.

Then you get a letter.

It's usually in the regular mail, mixed in with the utility bills and solicitations. You don't even have to open the letter for it to ruin your day. Seeing the IRS logo in the top left-hand corner of the envelope is enough to cause a sick feeling in your gut. You think of the last time you got pulled over by the police, or you recall a childhood memory of being summoned to the principal's office.

What did I do?

Now is not the time to panic. The IRS sends out millions of letters every year. As I mentioned earlier, most of them are relatively benign. They want to confirm some information or need you to supply additional information.

What you should absolutely, positively <u>never</u> do is ignore one of these letters. That's not to say that you need to reply (as is the case with the letter you probably got about a forthcoming stimulus check when you'd already received said check). Know that if they do request that you reply with a particular form or more information within a certain period of time, well, it's not really a request. Don't toss the letter thinking they'll forget about it. They won't. In many cases, not responding by the deadline is the same as confirming the veracity of the IRS's assessment of your return, and you can forfeit your right to contest their numbers later. This happens all the time. Of course, if you owe them money, not responding on time can cost you more money. That happens all the time too.

Virtually every piece of correspondence you receive from the IRS will be identified—usually in the top right-hand corner of the first page—by a number beginning with either CP (computer paragraph) or LTR (letter). The former designates a notice; the latter designates a letter (obviously an abbreviation rather than an acronym). As is the case with many bureaucratic idiosyncrasies, one would be hard-pressed to determine the difference between a "notice" and a "letter" from the IRS. Their correspondence is almost always some sort of notice, and it always comes in the form of a letter. It doesn't really matter. They all carry equal weight.

Regardless of which one you receive and regardless of whether or not you're required to reply, you should keep all correspondence from the IRS. Save it with the copy of your tax return, which you should always keep.

Below are some of the more common notices and letters and what you need to know about each. As always, help is just a phone call away: (833) 477-4778.

> CP3219A: We have determined that there is a deficiency (increase) in your 2020 income tax. You have the right to challenge the increase in US tax court. This notice explains how the additional amount was calculated and how you can challenge the increase in US tax court.

This one means that the IRS has received information (usually from an employer or your bank, but it can also be through third parties—more on that in the next chapter) that is different from what you reported on your tax return. You either paid too much or too little. Usually the latter. You've got ninety days to reply.

Pull out your copy of your tax return and compare it with the numbers they're showing you. If you agree with their assessment, fill out the attached form and send it in with your payment (remember that there will already be added penalties or interest or both). If something seems off, you'll need to reply with an explanation of why it seems off, along with the supporting documentation.

If it seems really off, call me.

> CP2000: The income and payment information we have on file from sources such as employers or financial institutions doesn't match the information you reported on your tax return. If our information is correct, you will owe $___ (including interest), which you need to pay by ____, 2021.

This is kind of like the previous letter, except that the discrepancy comes not from new information but from the information they already have on file. Sometimes you'll get one of these and the CP3219A. Sometimes they'll have different numbers. Either way, you've got ninety days to respond.

If you're confused, call me.

> LTR531: We have determined that you owe additional tax or other amounts, or both, for the tax year(s) identified above. This letter is your notice of deficiency, as required by law. The enclosed statement shows how we figured the deficiency. If you want to contest this determination in court before making any payment, you have ninety days from the date of this letter (150 days if this letter is addressed to you outside of the United States) to file a petition with the United States tax court for a redetermination of the deficiency.

This is your notice of deficiency. Again, if you agree with the amount they're showing, send it in within ninety days. If you don't, call me.

> LTR525: We reviewed your federal income tax return, any information you gave us, and made proposed changes to your tax. As a result, we found that you

____ are due a refund of $___

 X owe a balance of $___

This amount may include tax, penalties, and estimated interest due. You should pay the balance due immediately to avoid additional penalties and interest charges.

Known as a "general 30-day letter," this is a proposed adjustment to your taxes. I know, it sounds an awful lot like the previous notices. The main difference is that you only have thirty days to respond to this one.

To borrow a line from Ray Parker Jr.'s "Ghostbusters," I ask you, "Who you gonna call?"[3]

CP2501: The income and payment information we have on file from sources such as employers or financial institutions does not match the information you reported on your tax return.

---

3   Ray Parker Jr. "Ghostbusters." *Ghostbusters: Original Soundtrack Album*. Arista, 1984, vinyl.

This letter tells you specifically what income information the IRS received about you from others (including your employers, banks, mortgage holders, etc.) and that what you filed doesn't match that. It simply asks you to straighten out the discrepancies. You have the option (with a thirty-day deadline) to either agree with the information they have and allow them to calculate what you owe or to dispute their information and provide the documentation to back it up.

The disputing part is immensely trickier than the agreeing part. Call me.

LTR2205A&B: Your federal return for the period(s) shown above was selected for examination.

Guess what? You're getting audited! This letter (the A version is for individuals, the B for businesses) gives you all the details, including the name of the IRS agent assigned to your case.

Don't panic. Take a deep breath. Give me a call.

CP501: Our records show you have unpaid taxes for the tax year ended December 31, 2020 (Form 1040NR). If you already paid your balance in full within the last twenty-one days or made payment arrangements, please disregard this notice. If you already have an installment or payment agreement in place for this tax year, then continue with that agreement.

This is a notice that advises you (with no collection language) that there's a balance due. It's one of the most common notices taxpayers receive and is, to borrow a phrase from former president George H. W. Bush, among the "kinder and gentler" of IRS letters. In it, they also explain the taxes owed (including a due date), the amount due (including the interest and any penalties that have accrued), and the payment options that are available. It's probably also among the most frequently ignored IRS letters. As with most dealings with the government, the best time to dispute the amount they say you owe is early on. Even if you don't dispute what they say you owe, there are ways to lower those numbers, which we'll talk more about in chapter 8. In the meantime, go ahead and give me a call.

> CP502: Generally, the consequence of ignoring your CP501 letter (apart from possible added penalties and interest) is that you'll receive a CP502 letter. It's almost exactly like the CP501, except that you'll most likely see a higher "balance due" number on this one. That reflects the interest and penalties that have accrued since then. Sometimes the IRS will skip this one and go directly to:

> CP503: AMOUNT DUE: $___

As we notified you before, our records show you have unpaid taxes for the tax year ended December 31, 2016 (Form 1040A). If you don't pay $9,533.53 by _____, 2021, the amount of interest will increase, and additional penalties may apply.

This is technically the final reminder and will typically only give you ten days to respond, either with a dispute (or appeal request), a check, or by setting up a payment arrangement. The clock has been ticking since you received the first notice. The interest and penalties have been adding up since April 15 (filing extensions, as with those during the pandemic, notwithstanding). That clock is ticking louder now.

The IRS isn't going to forget about you. Your case isn't going to fall through the cracks or be ignored. When people say, "The only two sure things in life are death and taxes," this is what they're talking about.

Another sure thing in life: If you call me, I can help.

CP504: Amount due immediately: $____

This is a notice of intent to levy your state tax refund or other property. As we notified you before, our records show you have unpaid taxes for the tax year ended December 31, 2020 (Form 1040A). If you don't call us to make payment arrangements, or we don't receive the amount due within thirty days from the date of this notice, we may levy your property or rights to property and apply it to the $____ you owe.

While you may have been just a blip on the IRS radar through the course of receiving the CP501–503 notices, each step up the chain of letters/notices puts you into a smaller group of taxpayers and raised the level of interest the IRS has in you. The CP504 puts you in a whole new tier. You'll almost certainly receive this one via certified mail and, while those previous notices told you what the IRS might do, this one tells you what they're going to do. The line near the top, "notice of intent to seize (levy) your property or rights to property" says it all. Now it's not a threat—it's a promise.

The IRS is really good at keeping these promises. Unless you've simply been procrastinating and have no issue with the debt owed (and happen to have the amount due readily available), you should talk to a professional. That would be me.

> LT11/LT1058: Intent to seize your property or rights to property. Amount due immediately: $___. We haven't received a payment despite sending you several notices about your overdue taxes. The IRS may seize (levy) your property or your rights to property on or after _____, 2021.

Property includes:

- Wages and other income
- Bank accounts
- Business assets

- Personal assets (including your car and home)

- Alaska Permanent Fund Dividend and state tax refund

- Social Security benefits

This is your final notice via a certified letter. That ticking clock I mentioned? It's cranked up to eleven now. This is what the IRS is required to send you before they can actually do what they promised to do with the CP504. The LT11 will include Form 12153: Request for a Collection Due Process or Equivalent Hearing, which is how you file for an appeal—not of the debt itself, but of the collection process. We can help with that too.

We'll discuss these more in depth in chapter 8, when we talk about liens, levies, and wage garnishment (which is another type of levy). If you've received an LT11 or an LT1058 or both, you may want to skip ahead to that chapter. Better yet, call me now.

These are only a few examples. There are other letters you may receive throughout your journey to settling your tax debt, but these are among the most common. As you can see, there are all sorts of redundancies that can be stressful and confusing. It doesn't have to be either.

I may have mentioned that help is just a phone call away. My number is (833) 477-4778.

A note about scammers: They're everywhere. We hate them. There are things to keep in mind to avoid being a victim. Be aware that the IRS never initiates contact via email or phone. Once your case has progressed, you may get a call or email from the agent assigned, but even that's pretty rare. The IRS loves the USPS.

An IRS letter will have CP or LTR in the top right-hand corner. It's rare that a legitimate IRS letter won't include this. A scam letter will also often demand immediate payment of a debt—one that you apparently don't even know you owe. The IRS will always make multiple attempts to collect, and their Taxpayer Bill of Rights prohibits them from using aggressive language in their correspondence. A scam letter will usually state that you have to pay online—something the IRS would never do. Even if the letter seems legit, you can always call the IRS at (800) 829-1040 to confirm.

A good rule of thumb (not just for the IRS but for life in general): "When in doubt, check it out." You can find out more about IRS tax scams and how to report them at the government website usa.gov/irs-scams.

Chapter 5

"Why Me?" Audits 101

Different types of letters from the IRS tend to elicit different responses. Sometimes it's an expletive. Sometimes it's a groan. Sometimes (if you've overpaid), it's an "Oh boy!" Most often, it's a confusing "Huh?"

A dreaded 2205A or 2205B letter, informing you that you're being audited, usually prompts a combination of the above (minus maybe the "Oh boy!"), and it almost always evokes a "Why me?" Many times, the unfortunate taxpayer opening one of these letters already has an idea why, or at least a good guess. Perhaps there was income that should have been claimed but wasn't, or perhaps there was a deduction that shouldn't have been claimed but was. It's usually less a matter of "trying to pull one over on Uncle Sam" than a matter of thinking that the unclaimed income was no big deal or that the deductions were allowed. Too often, taxpayers will err on their own side, figuring that the IRS will simply correct any errors. This can be a risky and sometimes costly gamble. Remember, the IRS has up to three years to perform an audit. A red flag raised on your current tax return may inspire them to have a closer look at previous returns. Much better to err on the side of caution.

In this chapter, we're going to take a deep dive into audits: how they happen, why they happen, and what to do when they happen.

How the IRS Chooses Returns to Audit

Back in the days before computers were king and our entire lives were digitized, the IRS selected auditees using three methods:

1. Random

    The IRS would simply choose a certain number of returns from all the returns submitted. It was like winning the lottery but without the "winning" part.

2. Document Matching

    Document matching was really more related to document mismatching. If one or more of your sources of income filed a W-2 or 1099 (most common, although obviously there are more source-of-income forms) with your name and Social Security number, and you didn't claim that income, your chances of getting audited increased significantly.

3. Related Examination

Related examination occurred when you were already being audited. It meant that someone at the IRS had a funny feeling that errors or omissions on a current return might not be a fluke, and it might be worth taking a look at some of your previous returns.

Those last two still play a role in IRS audits. There's just little that is random about them anymore. Nowadays, they use what's called the "Discriminant Inventory Function System" (DIF). This probability-based analysis program scores tax returns based upon the likelihood of yielding additional revenue for the government. Each return is assigned a numeric score. The higher the score, the greater likelihood of being selected for an audit. A related program—the Unreported Income Discriminant Index Formula (you guessed it: UI DIF)—determines the likelihood that a return may contain inaccurate information or omitted revenue. The details of these programs are a highly guarded government secret that aren't even subject to Freedom of Information Act requests. The programs are based in part on the Taxpayer Compliance Measurement Program (TCMP) instituted in 1964 and regularly updated. The TCMP gathers data from a large sampling of tax returns to determine, among other things, regional and occupational norms relating to income and expenditures. For example, landscapers in

Florida make a whole lot more money than landscapers in rural Kansas, but they also have a significantly higher cost of living.

The DIF also looks at things like duplicate information (common with divorced couples who claim dependents) as well as certain deductions and credits that simply don't add up.

In the majority of cases, unless either DIF or UI DIF raises a flag, a real person will never even see your tax return.

Why the IRS Selected Your Return for an Audit

Okay. Your return was flagged. A real person *did* see it. They sent you a 2205A or 2205B letter.

Below are some of the most common answers to the question, "Why me?"

1. You goofed.

    It can be as simple as a typo or a misplaced decimal point. While you probably won't get audited for misspelling a word or forgetting to cross a t or dot an i, things like accidentally entering the wrong Social Security number or not double-checking your math can get your return flagged. Many times, you'll get a letter addressing the particular issue (an LTR2071C for the Social Security typo, one of a host of various forms for the math error), but not always.

2.   You fibbed about (or forgot) how much money you really made.

Underreporting income is one of the surest ways to get a real person to look at your return and send you a letter. I know, you didn't think it was that big of a deal. You only worked at that place for a few months, and your ex-girlfriend threw away the W-2 when they sent it to the apartment she'd thrown you out of. It was only a couple thousand dollars. You got most of what you paid in from your other job refunded, so you figured you were actually saving the IRS money by not including the lost W-2. Because that was easier than requesting a new one from the employer, and definitely easier than digging through your ex-girlfriend's apartment's dumpster.

Nice try.

This is a relatively innocent scenario and would most likely get you a CP3219A (notice of deficiency). But you never know.

What's more serious and can get you in a lot more trouble is if you attempt to get away with underreporting (or not reporting) income like tips or money earned from freelancing, from an independently owned business, or from any source, really. For unreported tips, you can get hit with a 50 percent penalty on the required Social

Security, Medicare, and railroad retirement taxes (as your employer was unable to withhold the required amount). With tips as well as with other underreported income, there's what's called an "accuracy penalty" of 20 percent. This applies if you're negligent or otherwise disregard IRS rules, substantially underpay your tax, claim tax benefits for a false transaction, or fail to mention a foreign asset.

But it can get much more serious than that. If you're found to have committed actual fraud, there's a penalty of 15 percent for each part of a month that your tax was late because of said fraud (up to 75 percent). There's also a second fraud penalty of 75 percent for substantially underpaying. And we mustn't forget about the $5,000 penalty if the IRS determines you submitted a frivolous tax return containing substantially unreported income.

These are just a few of the penalties that can be assessed. There are others, like actual jail time. That's rare, but it happens. Your best bet is to always remember that when it comes to dealing with the IRS, the truth may not set you free, but it's closer to free than the alternative.

3. We know you're charitable . . . but not that charitable.

Giving away stuff—whether it's money or clothing or household items—makes us feel good. It makes those who receive our gifts feel good. There's really no downside to charity (unless you get scammed). The IRS likes for you to give too, but they get suspicious if you seem to give too much. The average amount donated each year is about 3 percent of total income, though it varies based on income bracket. If your donations exceed that, the IRS won't think you're just an overzealous giver. You'll get flagged. You may get audited.

When deducting for your charitable causes, be sure to have written appraisals for any items you've donated, be sure to only give to nonprofit organizations that'll give you a receipt, and be sure to complete Form 8283 for any items valued over $250.

4. Your home is your castle—and your office.

Claiming deductions for a home office often raises flags with the IRS, mainly because it's so often done wrong. Here are some things you need to know:

Your home office has to be a space within your home used exclusively for your work, and it has to be your principal place of business. If you use a spare bedroom for work, but it sometimes doubles as, well, a spare bedroom (meaning that guests, you know, sleep there), you can't deduct it. Likewise, if you work on your laptop sitting on your sofa, you can only claim that space if you don't also watch TV or play video games there.

Generally, you'll have to file as self-employed (meaning you're paying the self-employment tax) or otherwise own your business in order to claim a home office. There are exceptions. For instance, you can claim a home office if you have self-employment income in addition to a regular primary job, but you can only deduct the expenses directly related to your self-employment.

Even though you can claim up to $1,500 for your home office, you can't assume that you qualify for the maximum deduction. It's not that simple, and automatically claiming the maximum could raise a flag.

5. You can write that off as a business expense.

Maybe so. Maybe not. The IRS defines an acceptable business expense as one that is "both ordinary and necessary." An ordinary expense is one that is common and accepted in your industry. A necessary expense is one that is helpful and appropriate for your trade or business. An expense doesn't have to be indispensable to be considered necessary. Advertising is a good example.

Remember, no matter what type of business you operate, the IRS has a code for it. That means they know which expenses are "ordinary and necessary." What's more, they know how much your type of business in your area typically spends on these ordinary necessities.

Be sure to keep those itemized receipts as well. If you went to Home Depot and picked up computer supplies for your office and a faucet for your kitchen sink, then deducted the entire amount of the receipt, it may have raised a flag.

6. If you don't make money at it, you might have yourself a hobby.

The IRS differentiates between a business and a hobby based upon a reasonable expectation of earning a profit. If you built a recording studio in anticipation of recording a hit song, even though you've never earned money as a musician or songwriter, it may be the IRS who "discovered" you. By all means, keep reaching for the stars—but don't try to deduct it.

7. Cash is king (except when it isn't).

If you run a small, mostly cash business, the temptation to underreport can be tough to resist. Resist it anyway. These types of businesses are among those most prone to audits. Not being diligent with your record keeping (perhaps forgetting that your bank also reports to the IRS) might explain that LTR2205B.

8. The red flag round up.

While the IRS requires you to round up or down to the nearest dollar, some taxpayers go a little crazy and round everything up (for deductions) and down (for income) to the nearest nice, neat number—like they were telling a friend. This is the reason you don't see the word "approximately" on tax forms. This may have been the red flag that led to your audit.

There are many other reasons the IRS singled you out for an audit. Usually, it's one of those listed above. Sometimes it's something else. Often it's a combination of things. A single red flag means a closer inspection; a closer look can mean more flags.

What You Should Do If You're Getting Audited

Okay, this is the easy one: Call me.

Seriously.

Audits can be complicated, stressful, and—above all—costly. Selecting that option for "audit representation" when you file your return with that tax preparation website will probably not be your best bet. You need a pro who knows exactly how to investigate and analyze the issue, present you with the best options (based upon your unique situation and an outstanding track record with the IRS), and resolve your tax problem at the lowest possible cost and without the burden of liens, levies, or garnishments.

That would be me.

Chapter 6

Contracting (and Subcontracting) Trouble

We've already touched on how the self-employed are among the most likely to fall under more intense scrutiny by the IRS. Returns are more complex for business owners, and it's easier to make a mistake—or several mistakes.

In this chapter, we'll dive deeper into some of the pitfalls of being your own boss. I'll help you avoid these pitfalls in the future and explain why you've been audited.

Contractor or Subcontractor? It's All Non-Employee Compensation to the IRS

If you're self-employed and work directly with a client to perform a job or service, you're a contractor. If, on the other hand, you're self-employed and your client is actually the person or company hired by the original client, you're a subcontractor. Probably the most common (and easily explainable) example is a homebuilder. The original client (the landowner) hires a contractor to build his or her dream home. The contractor then hires a variety of subcontractors (for roofing, wiring, etc.). To the IRS, it doesn't really make that much of a difference—contractors and subcontractors both fall under the umbrella of independent contractors. Here's what the IRS has to say about it:

> People such as doctors, dentists, veterinarians, lawyers, accountants, contractors, subcontractors, public stenographers, or auctioneers who are in an independent trade, business, or profession in which they offer their services to the general public are generally independent contractors. However, whether these people are independent contractors or employees depends on the facts in each case. The general rule is that an individual is an independent contractor if the payer has the right to control or direct only the result of the work and not what will be done and how it will be done. The earnings of a person who is working as an independent contractor are subject to self-employment tax.

Those earnings are classified as Non-Employee Compensation (NEC). Beginning in 2020, 1099-NEC is the type you should have received from your clients after providing them with a W-9, which includes your Social Security number or the somewhat confusingly named "Employer Identification Number" (EIN). The 1099-NEC replaces the 1099-MISC (which stands for "Miscellaneous," but I'm guessing you figured that out) that had been used previously in these cases. The latter is still used but more for things like royalties and rents and such.

There's a common misconception that payments made or received that are less than $600 "don't count." Don't fall for that. *All income counts*. You're simply not required to file a 1099-NEC for payments under that amount. Remember, even if the IRS doesn't have a record of payment attached to your Social Security number, they have multiple other means of figuring out your income (we discussed that earlier).

Also note that there are many different types of 1099s you may have to file with your return. The 1099-NEC is the one most applicable here. There's also a 1099-A (Acquisition or Abandonment of Secured Property), a 1099-S (Proceeds from Real Estate Transactions), and an SSA-1099 (Social Security payments), to name a few. These other 1099s have varying minimum amounts required to file, ranging from "any amount" all the way up to $100 million (that's the 1099-CAP, which is for Changes in Corporate Control and Capital Structure. You'll probably never get one of these, but it's still fun to know about).

Too Many Contractors, Not Enough Tax Revenue

If, as a small-business owner, you're the one doing the hiring, what follows is important.

It's become quite trendy in the twenty-first century to hire independent contractors rather than employees. The reasons are obvious. Independent contractors are responsible for their own taxes, which is way less complicated for those doing the hiring than having to do the withholding themselves. But, as quoted by the IRS above, there's a not-so-fine line between an independent contractor and an employee. A US Department of Labor study from a few years ago estimated that more than three million employees annually are misclassified as independent contractors. I'm sure it's even more today. That's millions of dollars of lost revenue for the government. They don't like that.

As with many IRS penalties, the severity is determined by intent. If you unintentionally misclassify a hire as an independent contractor rather than as an employee, three things can happen:

- You can be fined fifty dollars for each W-2 that you fail to file.

- You can face penalties of 1.5 percent of wages, 40 percent of Federal Insurance Contributions Act (FICA) taxes not withheld from employee, and 100 percent of the employer FICA taxes.

- You can face a "failure-to-pay" penalty equal to 0.5 percent of the unpaid tax liability for each month, up to 25 percent of the total tax liability.

If it's determined that you intentionally misclassified the person (or people) you hired, the penalties are more severe:

- You can face 20 percent of wages, 100 percent of FICA taxes not withheld from employee, and 100 percent of the employer FICA taxes.

- You can face criminal penalties of up to $1,000 per each misclassified worker.

- You can face up to one year in prison (rare, but possible).

So how can you tell for certain whether you're classifying your workers correctly? The IRS used to play Twenty Questions to determine employee-contractor status. These have now been streamlined into three broader categories:

① Behavioral Control

Do you have the right to direct and control how the worker does the task for which they were hired, through instructions, training, or other means? If you have to train the worker at all, you've got yourself an employee!

② Financial Control

Do you have a right to control the financial and business aspects of the worker's job, including how they get paid, how they make their services available, and the extent to which they have unreimbursed business expenses? If you can answer yes to any of those questions, you're a boss!

③ Relationship of the Parties

Is there a written contract, or do you provide employee-type benefits like insurance, vacation pay, or sick pay? Answering yes to the first doesn't necessarily rule out your worker being an employee; answering yes to the latter pretty much rules out independent contractor status.

To be more specific, an independent contractor will usually meet most of the following criteria:

- They'll operate under a business name.

- They'll have their own employees.

- They'll maintain a separate business checking account.

- They'll advertise their business's services.

- They'll have a contract with you describing your business relationship.

- They'll provide invoices for work completed.

- They have more than one client.

- They have their own tools and set their own hours.
- They keep business records.

If you're still unsure, the IRS is more than happy to help you out. Believe it or not, they have a form for that: Form SS-8, aka the Determination of Worker Status for Purposes of Federal Employment Taxes and Income Tax Withholding form.

If you think you may have accidentally classified an employee as an independent contractor, the IRS offers a way for you to fix it: the Voluntary Classification Settlement Program (VCSP). This allows you to reclassify your workers as employees for employment tax purposes for future tax periods with partial relief from federal employment taxes. To participate in this program, you have to meet certain eligibility requirements and apply to participate by filing Form 8952, the Application for Voluntary Classification Settlement Program. You also have to enter into a closing agreement (Form 906) with the IRS.

If this all seems complicated, that's because it is. That's why I'm here. Call me.

Section III:

Relief and Resolution

Chapter 7

Meet Your Friendly Tax Resolution Specialist

There are some people you'd rather not ever have to meet, at least on a professional basis. It's great to be friends with, say, a heart surgeon or a divorce lawyer, but you don't want to be a patient or a client. However, if and when you do need one of these professionals, you want the very best.

I have that kind of job. I'm one of the last people most taxpayers ever want to get to know, but I'm also the guy whom countless taxpayers are immensely grateful to have met. Nobody wants to have issues with the IRS. Everybody who does wants those issues resolved—preferably without property seizures or levies or wage garnishments. There aren't any scenarios in which those things don't suck.

Just as heeding the advice of your doctor can keep you from needing a heart surgeon, so too can hiring a good tax preparer keep you from needing me. But since you're reading this, that ship has most likely sailed. (Or as I've heard in the South, "That horse has left the barn.")

We've talked about the minefield that is the IRS tax code and the myriad of missteps you may have taken on your way to receiving one (or more) of their dreaded letters. Yet we've really only scratched the surface. There are as many unique tax situations as there are taxpayers. More situations, in fact, than there are IRS forms to specifically address. And that's saying something. Seriously, they've got *a lot* of forms.

I've mentioned that time is of the essence when it comes to dealing with the IRS, and that the best time to call me is after you receive that first letter. But that doesn't mean that it's ever too late to call. You may have thought the first letter was no big deal and not even opened it. This happens a lot. You may have crossed your fingers and hoped that the issue would go away or that the IRS would figure out that they made a mistake and eventually send you a note to apologize for any inconvenience they may have caused.

You may also wish for world peace and a winning lottery ticket. Probably not going to happen.

Winston Churchill was said to have remarked that you can always count on the Americans to do the right thing—after they have exhausted all the other possibilities. If he actually said that (and there's some dispute), it was kind of a low blow. Yet I think it applies, in a sense, to human nature in general. We don't like dealing with unpleasantness and will often do everything in our power to avoid confronting it. Seeking help with your IRS issues is doing "the right thing." Exhausting "all the other possibilities" first can be expensive.

Sometimes one of the barriers to reaching out to a tax resolution specialist is a feeling of guilt. You're the kid caught with your hand in the cookie jar. You're ashamed, usually at least a little embarrassed, and think that it's more honorable to concede and—more figuratively than literally in most cases—throw yourself on the mercy of the court.

Don't be ashamed. Don't be embarrassed. There are millions of words in the tax code, but "mercy" isn't one of them. ("Leniency" is one of them, but you have to know how to ask for it. There's a form for that.)

I've always called my office a No Judgment Zone—whether you're visiting in person or via phone or Zoom. I mean that with the utmost sincerity. I honestly don't care how you got here, except insofar as it relates to fixing it. You came to me because you need a voice, and I am that voice. I don't make judgments. My only concern is resolving your IRS issues; hence, the "resolution" in my job title.

What We Do: The Three Stages of Tax Relief

We've all heard about the five stages of grief: denial, anger, bargaining, depression, and acceptance. Although less tragic, the emotional roller-coaster ride of dealing with the IRS has some similarities to grief. There is denial of the seriousness of the letters, anger and depression at the threatened penalties, acceptance of the need for professional help. The stages are just streamlined and rearranged a bit.

Stage One: Analyze

When a taxpayer comes to me seeking help with the IRS, one of the first things we do—either face-to-face or virtually—is what I like to call "the letter ceremony." This is where we look at everything the IRS has sent you. As I've mentioned, it's usually more than one letter.

This is the first step of the analysis stage. As with your GPS, there's no way to lay out a map to your final destination—tax relief—without knowing the exact starting point. Your IRS letters tell us that. They also tell us how much time we have to get to where we're going and how hard we need to step on the gas. As a rule, the more letters you've received, the faster we have to go.

The next step of the analysis stage is an actual tax analysis. To use a medical analogy, this isn't a checkup, where your doctor takes your vitals and looks in your ears, nose, and throat. This is an examination. Your doctor pores over your medical records; I'll pore over your tax records—including everything the IRS has in their records pertaining to you. I'll use every means at my disposal, even a Freedom of Information Act request, if need be. It's a thorough and exhaustive investigation, and it's absolutely necessary to knowing exactly what your best options are.

Don't let this scare you. You're not going to have to go through your ex-girlfriend's dumpster looking for receipts. And as with your doctor—and the IRS—you're entitled to confidentiality. The National Association of Enrolled Agents (of which I'm a proud and upstanding member) has a stringent Code of Ethics and Rules of Professional Conduct. They—and I—take that very seriously.

Unlike with your doctor, your tax analysis won't require you to strip down to your underwear. And there definitely won't be any of that "turn your head and cough" stuff.

Stage Two: Present

This isn't "present" as in "gift" (although many of the taxpayers I work with view their newfound freedom from the IRS as such). After our thorough scrutiny of your tax situation, this is the stage where we present you with your best option to resolve your IRS dilemma.

Actually, I'll present you with several options that explain the pros and cons of each in a kind of cost-benefit analysis. But when it comes right down to it, there'll only be one best option—the one that resolves your issue at the lowest cost and prevents wage garnishment or property seizures or levies.

Stage Three: Solve

I love this part of my job. Once we've decided on the best solution to your dilemma, I make an offer to the IRS. I don't play guessing games. If I believe I can get the IRS to settle your case for pennies on the dollar, it's not a shot in the dark but based on my years of experience with situations similar to yours. As I've mentioned, I currently have a 100 percent success rate when it comes to my offers to the IRS being accepted. I don't offer them too much, and I don't offer them too little.

Our job isn't done after the IRS accepts the offer. We'll also do periodic checkups of your tax situation, keeping tabs on your IRS records so that any trouble that might be heading your way doesn't catch you by surprise. We'll often catch a new flag in your tax records before an agent does.

Analyze. Present. Solve. That's what we do. Our only objective is solving your tax problems, giving you your freedom, and setting you free from the shackles of the IRS.

That's real, honest-to-goodness tax relief.

Chapter 8

Un-digging the Hole

You know about your rights when it comes to dealing with the IRS. You know the facts (and the myths) of what may have led to the dilemma in which you find yourself. You've got an overall idea of what I do as a tax resolution specialist to help you navigate the often-turbulent waters of getting your dilemma resolved. These are all parts of the big picture—the photo on the box of the 1,000-piece IRS jigsaw puzzle. I hope I've helped you see that the picture on this puzzle box has a warning label: DON'T TRY THIS AT HOME.

In this chapter, we'll take a look at some of the individual pieces of that puzzle and at the ways in which a qualified TRS can not only show you which pieces go where but help you make them fit, even if it requires pulling out our own jigsaw and reshaping those pieces.

Puzzling, I know.

1. Audit Representation

In chapter 5, we discussed the most common reasons your number came up. Now let's talk more about the process of being on the receiving end of this most dreaded of governmental proceedings and how having the right TRS can turn *stress* into *relief.* Turn your frown upside down, if you will.

Types of Audits

- Correspondence

Correspondence audits are by far the most common types of audits. Sometimes they're not even technically audits but can become audits if not handled correctly. In many cases, the IRS will request documentation verifying one or more aspects of your return, whether it be a source of income, a deduction, or claimed dependents. Other times, they'll be notifying you of an error in your calculations and (usually) letting you know that you owe them more money. We talked about those various letters in chapter 4.

If the requested documentation is readily available, or if you agree with their assessment regarding what they say you owe, you probably don't need me. Mail them the documents (to be on the safe side, you should send them via certified mail) or write them a check. If, however, you don't have the requested documents, don't agree with their calculations, or have a sinking feeling that the requested documents aren't going to quite jibe with the information on your return, call me. I'll take it from there (and I'm much easier to deal with).

- Office

An office audit is more serious. It means the IRS has enough significant questions about or issues with your return that they believe a face-to-face meeting is required. They don't take these lightly, and they don't do them that often.

I can't stress this enough: You never want to meet face-to-face with an IRS agent. And, with few exceptions, you never have to!

As I told you earlier, there are only three types of professionals legally allowed to represent you before the IRS: CPAs, tax attorneys, and enrolled agents (like me). If the issues with your return are serious enough that they've requested you come to their office, then they're serious enough that you definitely don't want to go to their office.

I'll go for you. In most cases, it'll be via video conferencing, which has become the norm since the pandemic.

- Field

A field audit means that an IRS agent wants to come to your home or place of business (usually the latter) to look at your tax records and documentation in person. It's one of the rare exceptions to what I told you about never having to meet an IRS agent face-to-face. As you can imagine, it can be extremely stressful. However, because you have the right to be represented to the IRS by a tax attorney, CPA, or enrolled agent—like me—I can often get your case transferred to a field office near me.

Don't go it alone!

- Line-by-Line

The line-by-line audit is the real "bogeyman" of audits, but it's also the rarest. You probably have a better chance of winning your state's lottery (depending on the size of your state) than being subjected to one of these.

A line-by-line audit is exactly what it sounds like. The IRS goes over your return line by line. Like the lottery, these returns are selected entirely by random (pretty much the only exception to what I told you in chapter 5 about how returns are chosen for an audit). Line-by-line audits are specifically conducted to provide the IRS with data that will be used to conduct future targeted audits. This means your return may not have raised any flags in their computer system at all. As you can probably guess, though, a line-by-line audit is much more likely to find errors or discrepancies.

Regardless of which type of audit you're facing, your best bet is to let me face it for you.

2. Currently Not Collectible (CNC)

If the amount the IRS claims you owe is accurate, and if you simply can't afford to pay it, you may qualify for CNC status. This will defer any payments until you are able to pay, and it will head off any liens, levies, or wage garnishments. It won't keep penalties and interest from being added to your IRS debt, and they won't actually put a lien on your home (if you're a homeowner), but they will attach a Notice of Federal Tax Lien, which will alert your creditors that you owe the IRS money.

In order to apply for CNC status, the IRS requires exhaustive details of your financial situation. These can include proof of monthly income (including pay stubs and bank deposits) and proof of living expenses (with receipts). They may also ask you to file a financial statement (Form 433).

The IRS is going to be looking at four areas regarding living expenses:

- Food, clothing, and other household-type expenses

- Out-of-pocket health care expenses

- Housing and utilities

- Transportation

One thing to bear in mind if you're considering CNC status is that the IRS knows the average living expenses in your area. They also don't allow any extravagances beyond the necessities. This means that if you're single and living alone in a three-bedroom home for $1,500 a month in rent, they're not going to allow that $1,500 in rent. They're going to look at the average rental cost for a one-bedroom apartment in your area and only allow that. The same principle applies to your monthly food bill and car payment or other transportation costs. You can't expect them to allow daily pizza deliveries, and if there's public transportation near your home, they're not going to consider Uber rides as necessary.

If you qualify for CNC status, the IRS will put what's called a "closing code" on your file. This is a dollar amount, based on your financial situation as detailed above, that acts as the threshold for maintaining your CNC status. They'll periodically pull your tax records and compare them to this closing code. Once your income exceeds it, they'll want to talk to you about setting up an installment plan. We're going to talk about that next.

3. Installment Plans

If the IRS determines that your income is above and beyond your actual living expenses but that you don't have enough to pay your debt all at once, they may set up an installment plan. These may be short term (120–180 days) or long term (monthly, until the debt, interest, and penalties are paid). The short-term plans usually have no "user fees" attached; the long-term plans usually do (although they may be reimbursed, depending on your situation).

This may seem fairly straightforward and maybe not something for which you'd need professional help, but nothing could be further from the truth. For one thing, the interest on a long-term installment plan can add up to 25 percent annually to your debt. If you owe a substantial amount, this can mean that your monthly payments are barely making a dent. An enrolled agent can negotiate a deal with the IRS that will lower your interest to 6 percent. There's even a way to stretch out your payments until the ten-year statute of limitations runs out. That can save you some real money as well.

The IRS takes these installment plans seriously. If you're more than thirty days late with a payment, you can expect to receive a CP523, which is a "Notice of Intent to Terminate Your Installment Agreement." This will give you sixty days to make things right. After that, you're kind of back to square one, unless you appeal.

I can help with all that.

4. Offer in Compromise (OIC)

    An Offer in Compromise is an agreement between you and the IRS that settles your tax liabilities for less than the full amount owed. Legend has it that the OIC program's roots go all the way back to the 1940s, when heavyweight champion and national hero Joe Louis fell way behind on his taxes. Tax rates had skyrocketed during the thirties and forties, with the top marginal rate climbing from 24 percent to 90 percent, and Louis had less-than-reputable men handling his financial affairs. The IRS, in conjunction with the War Department, proposed a "charity fight" to relieve Louis of his tax burden, but it was quashed by Southern Democrats in Congress. When Louis died in 1981, he still owed money to the IRS.

    The OIC program was officially made a law in the early seventies and has undergone substantial changes over the years. Most people didn't know much about it until the late nineties, when companies like American Tax Relief and JK Harris started running national TV ads and making outlandish claims about settling tax debt. Neither are in business any longer, and both were successfully sued—JK Harris by over twenty states' attorneys general (they settled for $6 million).

These were the types of businesses I mentioned near the beginning of the book that were mostly shut down by the Federal Trade Commission.

The IRS may accept an OIC based on one of the following reasons:

- Doubt as to liability

  If there's a genuine dispute as to the existence or amount of the correct tax debt under the law, you may qualify for an OIC.

  Doubt as to collectability

  This exists in any case where the taxpayer's assets and income are less than the full amount of the tax liability. In these cases, I promise you the IRS will do everything they can to set up an installment plan.

- Effective tax administration

  This is when there's no doubt that the tax is legally owed and that the full amount owed can be collected, but requiring payment in full would either create an economic hardship or would be unfair and inequitable because of exceptional circumstances.

Contrary to what some companies will still have you believe (although, thankfully, not nearly as many), the process of qualifying for an OIC is far from a cakewalk. In most cases, the IRS won't accept an OIC unless the offer is equal to or greater than the Reasonable Collection Potential (RCP), which is how the IRS measures the taxpayer's ability to pay. (They've got acronyms for *everything*.) The RCP includes the value of the taxpayer's assets, such as homes or other real estate, automobiles, bank accounts, and pretty much anything else of value. The RCP also includes anticipated future income less certain amounts allowed for basic living expenses.

This isn't to say that settling IRS debt for pennies on the dollar (or even for zero dollars) isn't possible. I've done it for taxpayers I work with many times (a few cases are in the next chapter). But you really have to know what you're doing—like I do. I've never had the IRS turn down an offer I've made on behalf of a taxpayer. The trick is knowing how much to offer. Figuring that out takes some knowledge and experience. I've got you covered.

5.   Penalty Abatement

I think it's safe to say that everyone dislikes penalties. They're kind of like taxes that way. There really isn't any desirable connotation, at least to those being penalized (or taxed). To the IRS, of course, both mean dollars. In 2020 (according to the IRS website), penalties meant nearly thirty-two *billion* of them.

There are over 150 different penalties under federal tax law, for everything from filing late and paying late to errors on returns that led to underpayment and a host of other "noncompliant activity." Only three of those, however, make up the majority of penalties imposed by the IRS:

- Failure-to-File Penalty

  Forgot to file? Maybe it was too big a hassle and you guesstimated that you were probably okay. It's common sense that almost no one who's due a refund fails to file. Those who actually paid the exact amount of federal taxes throughout the year account for less than 5 percent of taxpayers. That means that if you didn't file a return, you most likely owe money, which means a penalty.

  The penalty for failing to file is 5 percent per month on the amount you owe, up to a maximum of 25 percent. This is, naturally, in addition to the amount you owe plus the interest on both the amount you owe and the penalties. The interest rate is the federal short-term tax rate plus 3 percent (for a total of 6 percent, as per this writing).

  Also note that the interest rate is compounded daily. No, this doesn't mean that 6 percent is added every day; it means that 1/365 of 6 percent is added every day. I know that doesn't seem like much, but it can add up. Especially considering that any amount added to your debt is then itself charged interest.

Without professional help, this can all add up quickly.

- Failure-to-Pay Penalty

If you filed on time but haven't paid what you owe, the IRS will happily add 0.5 percent per month of the balance due, up to a maximum of 25 percent. Interest will be compounded daily on all this as well. And guess what? The failure-to-file and failure-to-pay penalties are two separate penalties.

Without professional help, that can add up even quicker.

- Estimated Tax Penalty

The estimated tax penalty is for business owners (whether sole proprietor, partner, or shareholder) who have a tax liability each year of over $1,000 and are therefore required by the IRS to make quarterly estimated tax payments. The penalty for underpaying or failing to pay is equal to the interest lost by not having sufficient withholding or paying estimated taxes throughout the tax year. You know, "plus interest." In 2019, this one only accounted for 16 percent of IRS penalties. If it does apply to you, though, call me.

The good news is that the IRS is kind enough to occasionally allow what's known as "penalty abatement." The most common type is kind of a one-shot deal (technically known as the "First Time Penalty Abatement program"), and it requires meeting the following conditions:

- You didn't previously have to file a return, or you have no penalties for the three tax years prior to the tax year in which you received a penalty.

- You filed all currently required returns or filed an extension of time to file.

- You have paid, or arranged to pay, any tax due.

Penalty abatement is also possible for what the IRS deems "reasonable cause":

- Fire, casualty, natural disaster, or other disturbances

- Inability to obtain records

- Death, serious illness, incapacitation, or unavoidable absence of the taxpayer or a member of the taxpayer's immediate family

- Other reason that establishes that you used all ordinary business care and prudence to meet your federal tax obligations but were nevertheless unable to do so

Penalty abatement is also available if the IRS gave you the wrong information, either over the phone or in writing. These "statutory exceptions" are almost unheard of these days.

As with almost everything I've talked about in this book, there are forms available for you to do it yourself. But why would you?

6. Innocent and Injured Spouse Relief

Married taxpayers will often choose to file a joint tax return. There are significant benefits to filing this way, including the ability to deduct a higher amount of income, combining exemptions, and qualifying for more tax credits. But there's a catch. When filing jointly, both taxpayers are "jointly and severally liable" for the tax (basically meaning that you owe what they owe), as well as any additions to tax, interest, or penalties that arise from the joint return. Thus, both spouses on a married filing jointly return will generally be held responsible for all the tax due—even if one spouse earned all the income or claimed improper deductions or credits.

Divorce doesn't eliminate that liability. Remember, the IRS has up to three years to assess additional taxes and penalties on a return. So even though you legally split with that lying, tax-cheating spouse two years ago, you can still be liable for the consequences of your spouse's dirty tax deeds on returns filed while you were together—even if your divorce decree states that your ex will be responsible for any amounts due on previously filed joint returns. It doesn't seem fair, I know, but it's true.

Whether you're an "innocent spouse" (your spouse or ex-spouse failed to report income, reported income improperly, or claimed improper deductions or credits and now you're liable for it) or an "injured spouse" (the IRS took your refund to offset the aforementioned dirty deeds of your spouse), there's relief available. For the former, we can get debt relief; for the latter, we can actually get you that refund.

7. Wage Garnishment

You work hard for your money. The IRS works hard for your money too. Wage garnishment (or a "wage levy," as the government calls it) is often their last resort. By the time you get an LT11 or Letter 1058 (sent by certified mail to your address on record), you've already received many letters—including, most likely, CP501 through CP504 (in escalating order from "You owe us money" to "We said you owe us money" to "You owe us money now" to "We're going to get our money"). You may have stuck them, unopened, in a drawer. You may have read them and tossed them in the trash. You may have just put off dealing with it.

You'll want to deal with it now. Right now.

When you receive your LT11 or Letter 1058, you'll have thirty days before your employer also gets a letter from the IRS. Theirs will include a "Statement of Dependents and Filing Status" form for you to fill out, accompanied by a chart that will tell them not how much of your paycheck the IRS is getting, but rather how much of your paycheck you get to keep.

It's important to note that while most other creditors are allowed a maximum of 25 percent of your earnings, the IRS isn't most other creditors. They let you keep a certain amount—your "exemption"—based on your dependents and filing status (hence the aforementioned form), but that's it. If you make a decent living, the amount of your paycheck you get to take home can be significantly less than 75 percent. And it gets better. Because your employer is only allowed to pay you that specified exemption, any bonuses you receive will be applied to your debt. Another way that the IRS differs from most other creditors is that they don't need a judge's permission to do any of this stuff.

It's never too late to get relief from your IRS debt. It does, however, become more complex—and urgent—with each successive step along the path between "You owe us money" and "We're going to get our money." You need help to "head 'em off at the pass," as they say in the old cowboy movies.

8. Tax Lien Removal

Layfolk often confuse the terms tax liens and levies. They are related, in that the IRS uses them as mechanisms to get the money you owe them, but they're more part of the overall collection process. The lien usually comes first.

A tax lien, which the IRS makes public record via a Federal Notice of Tax Lien to alert your creditors, is an amount the government claims on an individual's property or assets or both to secure tax payments. This gives the IRS the rights to sell your property and claim tax payments from the proceeds. It doesn't mean they're going to sell your stuff; it just means they can. You get to keep your property or possessions, but you can't sell them or use them for collateral on a loan. A lien also covers future assets acquired during the duration of the lien. Unless you get the lien removed, it will remain in effect until the debt is paid in full.

There are a few ways an IRS lien can be removed:

• Pay Your Debt

Well, yeah. The IRS doesn't want to place a lien on everything you own. They'd much prefer you settle the debt, make arrangements, etc. As with so many of the more drastic measures the IRS will eventually take, liens and levies usually occur because the taxpayer has ignored all the warnings.

- Discharge of Property

A discharge removes the IRS lien from a specific property. This is for taxpayers who need to sell, refinance, or use their property as collateral for a loan that won't fully pay the tax debt.

- Subordination

Subordination doesn't remove the lien but allows other creditors to move ahead of the IRS, which may make it easier to get a loan or mortgage.

- Withdrawal

A withdrawal removes the public Notice of Federal Tax Lien and assures that the IRS is not competing with other creditors for your property; however, you are still liable for the amount due.

- Call Me

This one's the simplest and most effective. There are many ways beyond those mentioned above that we can help you get that lien removed and your tax debt settled. We offer freedom from the IRS for you and your property.

9. Tax Levy Release

A tax levy is more serious than a lien and, unlike a lien, doesn't require a court order. A levy means the IRS is actually seizing your property, assets, or wages. This is the part where they take your house and bank accounts. If you receive Social Security payments, they'll levy those too. They really, really want their money.

You'll receive the same LT11 or Letter 1058 via certified mail as you will for a wage garnishment and, again, if you've simply been procrastinating, the time to quit doing that is now! Once the thirty days allowed from the receipt of the LT11 or Letter 1058 have expired, the clock starts ticking even faster. Within days, the IRS will calculate a minimum bid price for your property. They'll provide you with a copy of the calculation and give you an opportunity to challenge the fair market value determination. They'll then give you the notice of sale and announce the pending sale to the public, usually through local newspapers or flyers posted in public places. After giving public notice, the IRS will generally wait at least ten days before selling your property. Money from the sale pays not just for the tax debt itself but for the cost of seizing and selling the property. If you've got money in the bank, those funds are held for twenty-one days before being sent to the IRS.

If you've received an LT11 or Letter 1058, stop reading and call me now! We can help you get those levies released, but it's much more difficult to "head 'em off at the pass" once they're past the pass.

10. Settlement

Settling your debt with the IRS is, of course, what this entire chapter has been about. It's really what this book is about. It simply means coming to an agreement with the IRS to resolve your tax debt for a lower amount than what they say you owe. We've covered a few of the tools that can be used as well as many of the means they'll use.

You'll see lots of ads for companies guaranteeing you that they can settle your case for pennies on the dollar. Nowadays, they have to be careful to post their fine print disclaimers (most of which go by faster than most humans read) saying that they can't really guarantee anything. The reason for this is simple. No matter how many hundreds of forms the IRS has (and we've only made a dent), there are as many unique tax situations as there are taxpayers. It's kind of like fingerprints or DNA.

The resolution of your tax situation is like a jigsaw puzzle, and we all know that it's a heck of a lot more difficult to put the puzzle together without the picture on the box. I've spent my career helping people like you put the puzzle together, and it all begins with being able to see that picture.

I've mentioned it before, but it bears repeating (and not just because I'm quite proud, although I am): As of this writing, the IRS has accepted 100 percent of all offers I've made on behalf of taxpayers.

So let's look at a few real-life cases.

Chapter 9

Real Taxpayers, Real Cases

You know your rights. You know about the myths, the letters, some of the missteps you may have taken, and the ways in which I can help free you from the shackles of your IRS debt. So now let's look at some real-world cases. Each of the following is a true story, with the names changed to protect the innocent taxpayers I represented.

A 401(k) Conundrum

Because contributions to retirement accounts, like a 401(k), are tax-deductible, when you withdraw money, the IRS considers it income. All of it. If that puts you in a higher tax bracket, you could wind up owing thousands more than you may think—including penalties and interest.

Like $20,000 more.

That's what happened to my friend John.

John was elderly and in ill health. His prognosis wasn't good. With the idea of alleviating as much financial burden as he could for his wife in the event of his passing, he thought it'd be a good idea to pay off his mortgage. He took the money out of his 401(k). Then John got a letter from the IRS (insert letter code) telling him he owed the government a whopping $20,000. As you can imagine, he was crushed. Poor health is stressful enough. Poor health and a huge, unexpected debt to the IRS was almost more than he could take.

At first, he was paralyzed with fear. He thought it must be a mistake—or worse, that it wasn't. He was devastated. As so often happens in cases with the IRS, he simply didn't know he had options. After John received his CP504 letter (the notice of intent to seize—levy—your property or rights to property), he came to me. His home was all he had. If he passed, it was all his wife would have. He'd worked too hard all his life to leave her homeless.

I immediately filed an appeal. As I worked on his case, I called him regularly to give updates of our progress. He confided to me that each time I called, he would start shaking, such was his worry that I had bad news. Each time I called, I put his fears to rest. Finally, I was able to call John with great news. Using the Effective Tax Administration type of an Offer in Compromise (based on John's exceptional circumstances), we were able to settle his tax debt for one dollar.

Most taxpayers I work with aren't facing such a perfect storm of catastrophic health issues and tax debt, but that doesn't make a big IRS bill less stressful or overwhelming. Call me. I can give you peace of mind.

That's one of the coolest things about my job.

1099 Troubles

When Brad was eighteen years old, he got a job that erroneously classified him as an independent contractor. Rather than withholding his taxes and sending him a W-2, they sent him a 1099. He was practically still a kid and didn't give it his due diligence.

In fact, he forgot all about it.

By the time Brad was in his mid-twenties, he'd gotten married, and he and his wife were raising two children. Like many young couples, they were barely making ends meet. So when the IRS sent him a bill for $18,000, he was floored. He and his wife's yearly combined income wasn't much more than that.

Remember, the IRS can only audit your tax returns for up to three years, but they have ten years to collect a debt (and, as we learned earlier, even that can be extended). Brad was still several years from reaching any statutes of limitations, and the interest and penalties from his original debt were continuing to mount. So Brad came to me.

I appealed his case to the IRS and did a detailed financial analysis of Brad and his wife's assets, income, and cost of living. It was obvious that Brad was unable to pay such a huge debt, and forcing him to do so would cause egregious hardship to his innocent wife and children.

The IRS isn't the enemy, and they're not villains. They may seem impersonal, but that's going to happen with any agency that deals with almost every adult in a country of 330 million.

I made an offer to settle Brad's case for one dollar.

The offer was accepted.

Bad Advice

Gus and Maria were another young couple I was able to help. Gus was going to school online, working during the day as a coffee machine technician. Maria was a stay-at-home mom, mainly because the cost of daycare would've taken most (if not all) of any income she may have been able to bring in. Maria handled the family's taxes and made the mistake of going to one of those pop-up tax preparation services you only see at tax time. The next thing Gus and Maria knew, the IRS was sending them a bill for nearly $30,000.

Young couples like Maria and Gus (or Brad and his wife) often think that because they don't make a lot of money, their options for resolving issues with the IRS are severely limited. They think their only recourse is to handle it themselves, which is almost always the wrong solution. Thankfully, they came to me. I wasn't able to settle their case with the IRS for a dollar, but I was able to settle it for $200—still a far cry from the nearly $30,000 original debt.

Gus and Maria send me Christmas cards every year.

When the Boom Busts

My friend Jeremy was a successful realtor during the boom years from the late 1990s through 2009. He built upon that good fortune with stock market investments and—as is the way of many people who make a lot of money—he spent a lot of money. When the bubble burst in 2008 and the country went into a major recession, Jeremy lost almost everything. He became depressed, and for a few years, he kind of stuck his head in the sand, failing to file taxes because he knew he'd never be able to pay them.

As we know, if you don't file your taxes, the IRS will calculate them for you. By the time Jeremy was ready to face the music, he owed the IRS nearly $2 million. That's when he came to me. Through a thorough analysis of Jeremy's finances, I was able to determine that the IRS, in their own calculations, had failed to consider either Jeremy's expenses or his market losses. Based on our analysis, we were able to show that Jeremy's actual debt was closer to $90,000—less than half of what the IRS claimed he owed. But even that was more than Jeremy was realistically able to pay. Through an OIC, we were able to lower his debt to $23,000, or just over 1 percent of the original IRS bill.

An Unsettling Settlement

Since 1949, every state in the union has had Workers' Compensation, an insurance program funded through payroll deductions that serves as a safety net in the event that an employee gets sick or hurt on the job and is no longer able to work. Like many insurance settlements, getting Workers' Comp can be an arduous and time-consuming process, taking months or even years to resolve. Workers' Comp cases have become a cottage industry within the legal profession.

If you receive a Workers' Comp settlement, whether as a lump sum or in regular disbursements, that money is fully tax exempt. At least it's supposed to be.

My friend Rosa came to me with an IRS letter saying that she owed $17,000 in taxes, interest, and penalties on a $50,000 lump-sum Workers' Comp settlement she received after she'd been hurt on her job and could no longer work.

How could this be?

It was all a mistake. Rather than sending her an insurance settlement statement, her former employer sent her a W-2. The IRS viewed her $50,000 Workers' Comp settlement as income. On paper, this might seem like an easy fix: inform the IRS of the error, and it goes away, right? Unfortunately (as you've seen by now), "easy" and "IRS" are words you'll rarely find in the same sentence. Or paragraph. I'm not even sure the word "easy" is found in the thousands of pages of the IRS tax code. Maybe it's in there somewhere.

Dealing with the IRS is a complex, multifaceted endeavor, and I don't recommend that anyone, apart from an experienced tax professional, try it on their own. In Rosa's case, I had to gather and submit all the court documents showing that her lump settlement was indeed a Workers' Comp settlement and that, rather than owing $17,000, Rosa should owe nothing.

Rosa's case is still ongoing. Sometimes the IRS wheels turn slower than usual (and slow seems to be the IRS's default setting). When all is said and done, I fully expect that my offer of zero dollars will be accepted.

My offers—at least as of this writing—are always accepted.

Conclusion

In today's internet age, almost all the information you think you'll ever need is at your fingertips—merely a few clicks (or if you're on your phone, taps) away. The IRS has detailed instructions on how to deal with almost any tax situation on their own website, and there are thousands of articles and blog posts with the same information.

Yet just as you wouldn't read a few articles and watch a few YouTube videos before removing your child's tonsils, neither should you rely on the internet to help you resolve your tax issues. It's extremely complicated and can get messy. Somebody could get hurt.

In other words (as with a tonsillectomy), don't try this at home.

As I stated from the beginning, my goal with this book was to try to remove the anxiety and confusion from dealing with the IRS, to debunk some myths, to explain your rights and options as provided within the 75,000 pages of the US tax code, and to emphasize and illustrate the need (and your right) to not go this alone.

If I've succeeded in my mission, I'd love for you to drop me a line at jesus@freedomtaxresolution.com.

If you've found you need help to relieve your stress, reduce what you owe, and regain your freedom, give me a call.

You've got my number.

About the Author

 With nearly three decades in the fields of tax preparation and tax resolution, Jesus Abikarram has made it his life's mission to help taxpayers navigate the complex and often confusing waters of IRS tax debt.

As an enrolled agent (the only professionals authorized to represent taxpayers before the IRS, along with CPAs and tax attorneys) and a member of the National Association of Enrolled Agents, the National Association of Tax Professionals, and the American Society of Tax Problem Solvers, Jesus utilizes his experience, knowledge, and love of helping people to analyze, investigate, negotiate, and—most importantly—resolve IRS tax issues.

As of this writing, his offers on behalf of the taxpayers he represents have a 100 percent success rate.

Licensed to practice in all fifty states, Jesus makes his home in Hallandale Beach, Florida.

Expert
Press
www.ExpertPress.net